Title Page: Budgerigars in outdoor area of aviary. Photo by Walter D. Verizzo.
Front Endpapers: White-headed nuns. Photo by Harry V. Lacey.
Back Endpapers: Lovebirds. Photo by Glen S. Axelrod.
Front Cover: Photo by Glen S. Axelrod.
Back Cover: Photo by Dr. Herbert R. Axelrod.

Originally published in German by Franckh'sche Verlagshandlung, W. Keller & Co., Stuttgart/1976 under the title *Kafige und Volieren.* © 1969, 1974 by Franckh'sche Verlagshandlung.

ISBN 0-87666-840-6

Distributed in the U.S. by T.F.H. Publications, Inc., 211 West Sylvania Avenue, PO Box 427, Neptune, NJ 07753; in England by T.F.H. (Gt. Britain) Ltd., 13 Nutley Lane, Reigate, Surrey; in Canada to the pet trade by Rolf C. Hagen Ltd., 3225 Sartelon Street, Montreal 382, Quebec; in Canada to the book trade by H & L Pet Supplies, Inc., 27 Kingston Crescent, Kitchener, Ontario N28 2T6; in Southeast Asia by Y.W. Ong, 9 Lorong 36 Geylang, Singapore 14; in Australia and the South Pacific by Pet Imports Pty. Ltd., P.O. Box 149, Brookvale 2100, N.S.W. Australia; in South Africa by Valid Agencies, P.O. Box 51901, Randburg 2125 South Africa. Published by T.F.H. Publications, Inc., Ltd., the British Crown Colony of Hong Kong.

CAGES AND AVIARIES

Curt af Enehjelm

TRANSLATED BY U. ERICH FRIESE

This well-kept aviary, designed for the southern California climate, is used for breeding grass parakeets. Photo by Chelman & Petrulla.

Opposite: Violet-necked lory, *Eos squamata riciniata*, on nest box perch in outdoor aviary. Photo by Ray Hanson.

Large flight cage for budgerigars, among other cages in a bird room.

Contents

A sliding bottom tray facilitates cleaning and replenishing the grit covering. Photo by Louise Van der Meid.

Opposite: Cage birds such as this cockatiel can be put outside in warm weather as long as they are not placed in direct sunshine. Photo by Ray Hanson.

11

Several sizes and styles of cages are used here to house a cockatiel, a yellowhead parrot, and Fischer's lovebirds. Photo courtesy of Don Rowland.

ALL ABOUT CAGES

How the bird keeper accommodates his birds depends largely upon the space available. Not every enthusiast has a room that can be devoted entirely to birds nor does he have an outside aviary with an adjoining enclosed room. Many hobbyists have to settle for cages in lieu of aviaries, and even the owner of the most elaborate bird facilities cannot completely dispense with cages. There are always situations where it is necessary to place birds in cages; for example, to isolate newly arrived or diseased birds for observation and quarantine, or to separate incompatible birds. Yet, even if the hobbyist is forced to keep birds exclusively in cages, a great deal of success can be achieved if suitable cages are available and also if the species chosen are suitable for cage maintenance (not all birds are).

A cage can never be too large, and one that is flat on all sides, rectangular in shape and longer than it is high gives birds the most freedom of movement. The ideal relationship between length, width and height should be the ratio of 4:2:3 (fig. 1). This means that the width is about one-half of the length and the height about three-quarters of the length of the cage. These size relationships are especially important in smaller cages. Round, hexagonal or octagonal cages are generally less suitable than rectangular cages. The roof of the cage should be flat or may be slightly arched (fig. 2). If the cage is intended to be decorative indoors it can have a painted roof.

This decorative bamboo cage is adequate only for housing finches. Photo by Dr. M. Vriends.

Natural vegetation and a climbing chain provide interest for caged parrots. This cage is just big enough for the yellow-fronted Amazon, *Amazona o. ochrocephala.* Photo by Dr. Herbert R. Axelrod.

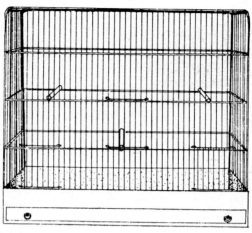

Fig. 1: Metal cage with straight roof. Note the practical location of the gates.

The cage must be securely attached to a stand and have an easily removable bottom tray. It is recommended that the base of the cage be about four inches high and the removable tray about two inches deep. This keeps sand and food from being scattered outside the cage.

Some models also feature "seed guards": strips of glass or plastic that are inserted into metal guides at the four corners outside the wire. It's also useful to install a hatch over the tray opening to prevent small birds from escaping when the tray is removed (fig. 3).

The bottom tray should fit as tightly as possible into the base frame in order to prevent sand and seed shells from falling between the frame and the cage base. For that purpose some cages have strips called dust strips sloping along the sides and just above the tray. If the bottom tray does not rest directly on the bottom of the cage but instead rests on small strips mounted slightly off the bottom, removal of the tray is made easier.

Cages can be open on all sides as can the roof (wire), or

16

Fig. 2: Cage with wood frame and slightly arched roof.

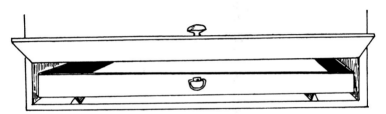

Fig. 3: Cage base with hatch. The tray is resting on narrow wooden supports.

they can be so-called crate cages, which have a wire front only. An open cage has a frame made of wire or wood. The wire front consists of thin, vertical wire strands. Also available are cages with horizontal wire strands.

Open cages are usually made with tin-coated wire which is quite practical. Brass cages have a tendency to turn green due to oxidation caused by splashing water. This can lead to poisoning when the bird picks at the metal. If rust appears, it should be removed by sanding, and then the cage should be recoated with a non-poisonous lacquer or plastic paint. However, parrot cages should not be painted; instead, after a thorough cleansing they should be plated.

17

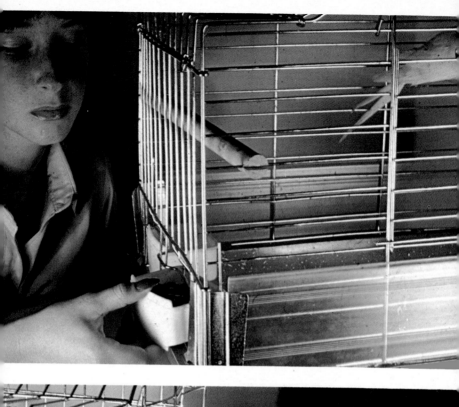

Large hinged doors afford easy access to all areas within a cage and also serve as perches for birds leaving or entering their cages. A strong latching device is necessary to prevent parrots such as this African grey from escaping on its own. Photo by Dr. Herbert R. Axelrod.

Opposite: Plastic "seed guards" on this cockatiel's cage can be removed when attaching food and water containers; then they should be replaced so that seed hulls and grit remain within the cage. Photos by Glen S. Axelrod.

Cages with a wooden frame are quite common, and there are several manufacturers who produce excellent models. The frame is usually made of beech and has a lacquer coating. Hobbyists often insist that wooden-frame cages offer better hiding places for parasites than metal cages. This is true only if the cages are not inspected often and not thoroughly cleaned. Modern insecticides available in spray cans make the destruction of parasites quite easy. However, during the application of these highly poisonous substances, the birds, the feeding containers and the bottom sand should be removed from the cage to avoid exposing the birds directly to the poisons.

It has been my experience that birds kept in cages made with a wooden frame do particularly well. The wire in these cages is made of tinned, galvanized or baked material, and the tray is made of sheet metal.

Some manufacturers supply cage kits which can be assembled by the hobbyist. They include drilled connecting straps, corner posts and straight wire. A handy hobbyist can thus construct his own cages in many different shapes and sizes.

Cages with a wooden frame are not suitable for parrots since these birds will chew through it in no time at all. However, this type of cage is especially suitable for finches and soft-billed birds.

The cage should always have a sufficient number of doors for easy access to all its areas and corners. In addition, large cages should have a large hinged door through which nest boxes and branches can be put into them. Smaller doors at the lower corners of the front—doors through which food containers can be placed on the bottom of the cage without disturbing the birds—are very practical in breeding cages. In addition, small doors can be located higher up in order to attach nest boxes to the outside of the cage or to inspect nests inside the cage. Most suitable for this purpose are easy sliding drop-gates.

The thickness of the wire bars and the size of the space between them depends largely upon the bird species to be kept in the cage. Most commercially available cages have a wire thickness of 1.4 to 1.5 mm and are spaced about ½-inch apart. Such thin wires are rather flexible—especially when the distance between the horizontal (cross) wire or wooden rods is large. The space between the wire rods must never be so large that a bird can force its head between them. This can easily happen when the wire is too thin and too pliable. The bird cannot pull its head back into the cage, and the result is obvious.

An Oriental-style cage with a wooden frame. The perches shown, however, are too large (and too few) for species suited to the cage size.

Note that this indoor flight has two doors. A person enters the enclosure and then closes the door before opening the second door to the aviary proper. This helps prevent the escape of birds. Photo by Dr. Herbert R. Axelrod.

Opposite, top: A double breeding cage for canaries. At the center are removable partitions. The plastic one is removed first, leaving a wire partition through which a male bird on one side may feed a female on the other side. For mating, the wire partition may be removed. The wire baskets are for nest building.

Opposite, bottom: Small cages are not normally recommended for conures, but they are excellent as carrying cages or hospital cages. Photo by Dr. Herbert R. Axelrod.

23

For very small finches the distance between the vertical wire rods should not be more than nine mm (with a wire thickness of 1.65 mm), and the distance between the horizontal supports should not exceed six inches.

Canaries, budgerigars and even larger birds can be kept in cages with a larger wire grid (distance ½-inch). However, the above-mentioned measurements provide greater utility for cages so that small as well as large birds can be kept in them. Moreover, the wire mesh is not too narrow to create an unappealing aesthetic effect when housing larger birds. There are cages commercially available in different sizes up to three feet long, which have a space of three-eighths inch between adjacent wires.

These are the general requirements for cages. There are, of course, other specific requirements for different bird species and special purposes which require specialized cages. Therefore one can distinguish between cages for small birds, breeding cages, flight cages, cages for birds feeding on soft foods, cages for canaries, for budgeriagars, for parakeets, for parrots, for quail and other ground birds. These will be discussed briefly later on.

These indoor cages were taken outside for the purpose of photographing them and their inhabitants. The eclectus seems to prefer perching on top of its cage. Photo by Kerry Donnelly.

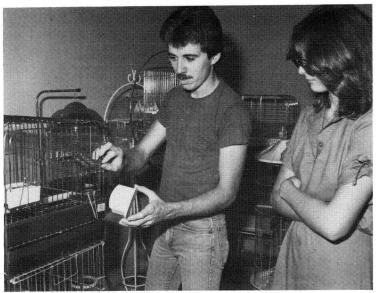

A knowledgeable person can help you select a cage of the size and style most appropriate for the bird species to be kept. Photo by Vince Serbin.

CAGE SIZES

The size of the cage needed depends upon the bird species to be kept and upon the purpose for which it is intended. Here are a few practical suggestions for sizes, considering some of the more common commercially available models. In all of these cases the measurements are to be taken as minimal sizes, and deviations of an inch or two are largely insignificant. The measurements are given in inches, and in sequence: length × depth × height.

(1) 19–23 × 12 × 16
(2) 29–31 × 16 × 19–23
(3) 35 × 16 × 19–23
(4) 39 × 16 × 23
(5) 47 × 19 × 23–31

Cages larger than the ones listed above can be considered indoor aviaries, and they will be discussed later.

25

Glass cages or converted aquariums may be used to provide a draft-free environment for newly hatched birds. This white cockatoo, *Cacatua alba,* 33 days old, has been enclosed for warmth and safety. Notice that the top of the enclosure has been left partially open to admit fresh air. Photo by Frank Nothaft.

A pair of pied peach-faced lovebirds as seen through the open door of their cage. Note that the wire mesh has a small rectangular pattern, rather than having long horizontal or vertical strands. Clips are used for holding the top and sides together in this homemade enclosure. Photo by Barbara Kotlar.

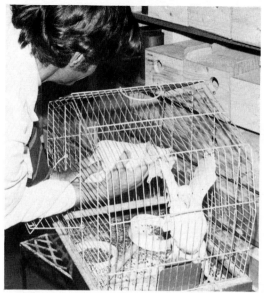

A cage this size, while obviously inappropriate for two parrots, may be useful for temporary housing as is being done at this New Zealand pet shop. Photo by Dr. Herbert R. Axelrod.

A flight cage can accommodate the following number of grass finches or other birds of similar size: Size 1: a single canary or budgerigar, a pair of waxbills, zebra finches or society finches; Size 2: two to three pairs; Size 3 or Size 4: four pairs; Size 5: five to six pairs.

Birds the size of Java rice birds can be kept in flight cages in the following numbers: Size 2: three to four birds; Size 3 to 4: six to eight birds; Size 5: ten to 12 birds. Larger birds, such as cardinals or grosbeaks are not very compatible in such confined quarters. Therefore, these are better kept individually. If they get along with each other single pairs can be kept in cages of Sizes 2 to 5.

Parrots really do not belong in cages; instead they should be kept in aviaries. However, if one is forced to keep these birds in cages temporarily, then a pair of the smaller grass parakeets such as the Bourke's or the turquoisine can be kept in pairs in cages of Size 4; larger species such as rosellas should be kept in cages of Size 5. Small-beaked parakeets, lovebirds and similar-sized parrots can be kept in pairs in cages of Sizes 3 or 4, even for breeding purposes.

BREEDING CAGES

Among grass finches there are many species that are suitable for breeding in cages. In particular, society finches and zebra finches can be bred in cages of Size 1, although Size 2 would be more satisfactory. I have bred grass finches, parrot finches, silverbills and similar forms in cages of Sizes 2 to 4. From among the African waxbills, fire finches, cordon bleus, St. Helena waxbills, aurora finches and gold-breasted waxbills will occasionally breed quite well in cages of Size 5. However, breeding often fails if these birds have previously been bred in larger indoor facilities. The same applies to some of the Australian species such as Gouldian, star, owl and parrot finches.

From among the finches, the green singing finch and some of the other African finches have often been bred in cages. Cuban, jacarini, saffron finches and hooded siskins have also been bred successfully in some of the roomier cages of Sizes 4 and 5.

As mentioned above, Australian parrots are totally unsuitable for cage maintenance, and even less so for breeding attempts. Somewhat less demanding are the South American species. Some of the smaller wedge-tailed and small-beaked parrots do rather well in larger cages of Sizes 4 and 5. These cages can also be used for breeding.

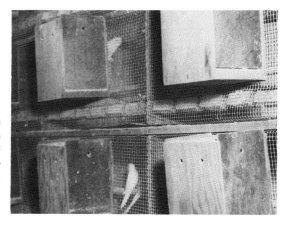

Nest boxes have been attached to the outsides of these budgerigar breeding cages.

30

Perches of different shapes are shown in this posed photograph of Gloster Fancy canaries.

Opposite, top: A clear plastic bathing container attached at the open door of a canary cage.
Opposite, bottom: This young mynah seems to prefer an open water container for bathing.
Photo by Louise Van der Meid.

The various species of wild pigeons and doves are hardly suited for cage maintenance and breeding. Only some of the smaller species such as diamond doves, cape doves, passerine ground doves and other species of a similar size can be successfully kept in pairs in cages of Size 5. They may even breed and raise young in these cages.

This parrot is housed—temporarily, one hopes—in a budgerigar show cage.

CAGES FOR SOFTBILLS

Individual males of these types of birds kept as "singers" can be housed in various commercially available cages. The following are general guidelines: Cages of Size 2 are suitable only for birds up to the size of nightingales, and cages of Sizes 3 and 4 are well suited for thrushes. Both types of cages should have a height of 20 inches. For soft-billed birds, it is best to use crate cages or half-opened cages, which have a solid back wall. The ceiling consists of a frame covered by a soft cloth or wax cloth. However, for my birds I use a solid ceiling which is covered on the inside with foam rubber; it is very soft. Such a soft ceiling is absolutely necessary in order to prevent the birds from becoming injured during a panic. It is mainly required for native softbilled birds or those from similar latitudes. Tropical forms, which are non-migratory, do not require a soft ceiling.

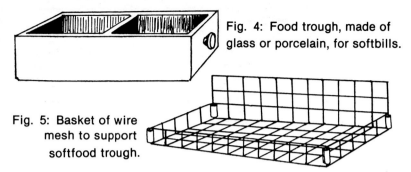

Fig. 4: Food trough, made of glass or porcelain, for softbills.

Fig. 5: Basket of wire mesh to support softfood trough.

Food containers, which should be attached at both narrow ends of the cage, should be elongated porcelain or glass troughs, about six inches long, three inches wide and 1½ inches deep. Often they consist of two compartments; this is useful when different types of food are to be offered simultaneously (fig. 4). These containers are put into the cage through openings in the front which are then closed off by metal slides. The food containers should be located at a small table or be securely tied by two wires—one underneath the container and the other along the side. For that purpose I use small "baskets" made of fine-mesh wire into which the food containers fit tightly. The sides of these baskets are only about one inch high (a little shorter than the food containers), so that the birds do not injure their feet when they are standing on the edge of the food container (fig. 5). Quite often hobbyists use an outside feeding technique whereby the food containers are attached to the outside of the cage on either side, and they slide into metal grooves (fig. 6).

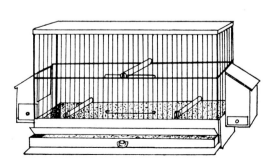

Fig. 6: Softbill cage with food containers attached to the outside.

33

White-fronted Amazon, *Amazona albifrons,* on hexagonal perch. Photo by Dr. John Moore.

Opposite: White cockatoo, *Cacatua alba,* allowed to perch atop its cage. Compare this specimen with the 33-day-old one on page 26. Photo by H. Lacey.

Water is best offered in customary plastic water dispensers. For several hours each day a bathing container should be placed against the door in the front of the cage. In order to keep water from being splashed against the wood rim below the door (to avoid deterioration of the wood), the rim is covered with a "saddle" in the form of a piece of aluminum sheet metal (fig. 7).

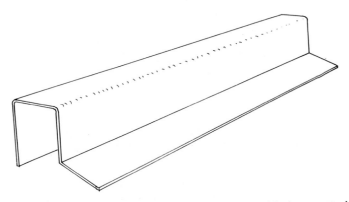

Fig. 7: Sheet aluminum "saddle" to protect wood below cage door.

The perches—two upper ones and two lower ones—must always be made of soft wood since most of the softbilled birds have very delicate feet. Ideally, perches should be made of debarked wood; these can be removed from the cage frequently and washed with hot water, or they can be completely replaced. These perches should be variably thick so that the birds are forced to change their grip as they change perches. Most commonly available sizes are from one-quarter to three-quarters of an inch in diameter. They should be placed sufficiently far away from the side walls so that the birds do not damage their tail feathers when turning around. For shama thrushes the perches should be positioned eight inches away from the walls. In these cages the perches should be parallel to the side walls,

36

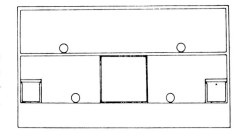

Fig. 8: Schematic drawing of perch positions in soft-bill cage.

attached in such a position as to afford the birds maximum space (fig. 8). Perches made from fired clay are used for blue and rock thrushes and, in addition, a few large stones are placed inside the cage. These birds develop swollen feet if they have only wooden perches available in their cages.

Perches of natural wood in a variety of sizes are appropriate for this rosella in a cage assembled with cage clips. Photo by Kerry Donnelly.

Black-capped lory, *Lorius lory somu,* climbing on the sturdy wire mesh of its enclosure. Photo by P. Leysen.

Opposite: Thick wire is necessary for species such as this Hispaniolan Amazon, *Amazona ventralis.* Photo by Cliff Bickford.

39

CAGES FOR GROUND BIRDS

Cages for quails, stilts, tits, larks and others are best equipped according to the same basic principles applied to softbilled birds. A soft ceiling is mandatory since these birds have a tendency to take off in a panic flight and so hit their heads on the cage ceiling. Cages of this type need not be excessively high; twenty inches is totally adequate. However, since some of these birds like to take sand baths, the cage should have a sufficiently large bottom area, with the tray deep enough to accommodate a thick ground cover.

The food containers—ideally, long troughs as used for softbilled birds—are placed on the bottom along the two narrow sides of the cage. Some species such as stilts and tits require perches; others such as quails do not.

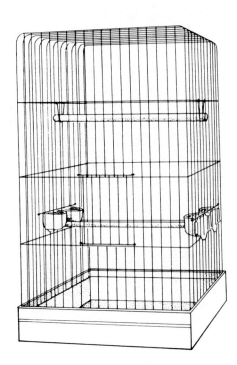

Fig. 9: Tall parrot cage with a small bottom area.

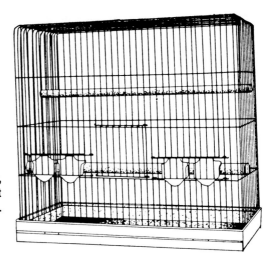

Fig. 10: Larger, rectangular parrot cage.

PARROT CAGES

For individually kept medium-size parrots and parakeets, such as cockatiels, Senegal parrots, red-tailed parrots *(Pionus)* and similar species, a standard cage of Size 2 is completely adequate. Of course, these species can also be kept in a standard parrot cage if it is not too small—a common fault among such cages.

Cages for large parrots, such as African greys or Amazons, should have a bottom area of twenty to twenty-five inches square and a height of about thirty inches. For reasons of space economy, relatively high cages which have a small bottom area are often used; in spite of this they are rather roomy (fig. 9). However, an elongated cage of Sizes 2 to 4 is actually better suited for parrots (fig. 10).

The largest parrot species such as macaws and cockatoos are not suited for cage maintenance. They do best in spacious aviaries. Cages for these species should have a bottom area of three feet by three feet and a height of four and one-half to five feet. Yet, even in these cages macaws tend to damage their long tails; this mars their appearance.

41

Scarlet macaw, *Ara macao,* climbing on cages that obviously are not suited for such a bird. Larger parrots need room to stretch their wings. Photo by Ray Hanson.

42

Parrots as large as the scarlet macaw are best kept on a stand. Photo by Ray Hanson.

Parrot cages must always be made completely of sturdy metal; otherwise, the parrots would quickly destroy them. The wire diameter for small species should be about 2 mm; for African greys and species of similar size the thickness should be about 3 mm; the space between adjacent cross members should be about three-quarters to one inch. Suitable cages for macaws are rarely ever available; instead, they have to be custom-made. For these birds the wire thickness must be at least 5 mm. However, it is simpler and often cheaper for the hobbyist to construct such cages himself from wire mesh having a thickness of about 3 mm. If the mesh is not too large—a three-quarters to one-inch opening—the macaws cannot bite through the wire.

Notice that the wire mesh provided for this macaw is backed by solid walls.

Quite often macaws and other large parrots are kept on stands only. Such a device consists of a perch that is twenty-five to thirty inches long and is attached to a vertical metal pipe (fig. 11). The perch must be easily replaceable. This device is then placed in the middle of a metal tray which is four inches long and 30 inches wide. The metal pipe would have a series of short cross bars down its length, to enable the macaw to climb up and down the pipe. Food containers for macaws can be attached either onto the perch or below in the metal tray. Quite often the birds are secured to the perch with a leg band attached to a chain. However, when macaws are unsupervised they should be placed inside a cage.

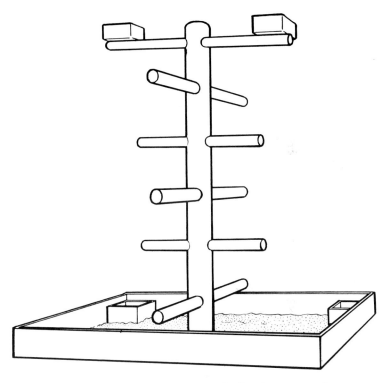

Fig. 11: Stand for macaws and other large parrots.

Male red-sided eclectus parrot, *Eclectus roratus polychloros,* using a horizontal chain as its perch. Photo by Dr. Herbert R. Axelrod.

Opposite, top: Note the wire mesh holder for food containers behind this female eclectus parrot, *Eclectus roratus.* Photo by John Daniel.
Opposite, bottom: A guard rail helps to prevent the inevitable spillage during feeding. Cockatiels, *Nymphicus hollandicus.* Photo by Dr. Gerald E. Allen.

The thickness of a parrot perch should correspond to the size of the birds being kept. A diameter of one-quarter to one-half inch is suitable for African greys and Amazons. A parrot cage should have two perches, each of a different thickness. Perches can be made of branches cut to size instead of dowels. However, parrots quickly chew up natural branches, so an adequate supply should be kept on hand. Metal rods should never be used as perches. If parrots are offered extra fresh branches and twigs to chew on, this will deter them from chewing on their own perches. The perches should be firmly attached and should be parallel to the walls. The distance between the perches and the cage walls should be large enough to prevent the birds from damaging their tail feathers. Perches should be attached at a height that is comfortable for the bird without permitting its head to collide with the cage ceiling. For instance, African greys require a distance of six inches to the cage wall and twelve inches to the cage ceiling. A swing, commonly found in most commercially made parrot cages, reduces the amount of space in the cage. The swing can be replaced with a ten-inch-long sturdy chain. Parrots tend to spend much time climbing up and down such a chain.

A swing further reduces the limited amount of space in this parrot's cage.

Although this yellow-naped Amazon seems to enjoy its freedom, it will not readily leave its perch because of clipped wings. Photo by Louise Van der Meid.

If a parrot will be permitted to move about freely, a perch can be attached on top of the cage; a tame bird then tends to spend much time on such a perch.

In cages for large birds it is important to have the food containers firmly attached and placed where they can be serviced from outside the cage. Most commercially available cages have only two food containers, and that is not enough. A parrot cage should have three, even four, food containers: two for large and small seeds, one for fruit and germinated seeds and one for water. These must be easily accessible from the perch.

The door of the cage should be located to provide access to all corners of the cage. Cages used for tame parrots should have doors sufficiently large, so that the bird can be removed while sitting on the hand of the keeper. A cage door should have a simple but safe locking device which cannot be opened by the bird.

Keeping budgerigars in good health will preserve the beautiful colors that careful breeding has created.

Food containers placed on the floor are welcomed by this brood of young Border Fancy canaries. Photo by H. Lacey.

A breeding pair of budgerigars in all-metal cage with nest box attached. The perch arrangement in this cage allows ample free space as well as easy access to food and water containers (at rear of cage) and to the hinged door. Photo by Louise Van der Meid.

BUDGERIGAR CAGES

Budgerigars can be kept in open, all-metal cages as well as in box cages. A cage of Size 1 is suitable for a tame, individually kept bird. For greater utility, the cage should have a rather large hinged door through which the bird—in the event it is permitted to fly around—can easily return to the cage. The budgerigar cage should be equipped with three to four perches of suitable thicknesses and possibly with some additional branches. However, the branches must not interfere with the flight area.

A cage of Size 2 or 3 is suitable for a breeding pair of budgerigars. Juveniles can be accommodated in cages of Size 5, with possibly six to eight birds to a cage. However, out of breeding season it is recommended that the breeding pair and the juveniles be kept in an outdoor aviary with an attached indoor enclosure. The breeding cage should have two perches, each of different thickness (7 to 15 mm), and they should be attached parallel to and about ten inches from the side walls. The nest boxes can be attached inside or outside the cage. In box cages it is more advantageous to attach the nest box inside, since attaching anything on the front of the cage would allow less light to pass into the cage.

In larger breeding facilities the cages are usually placed side-by-side or one on top of the other and arranged in rows. If a special bird room is available, it is more practical and cheaper to build solid compartments in three levels along one wall. When budgerigars are bred in cages, hobbyists should be cautioned against placing two or more breeding pairs together. This can provide many undesirable surprises such as fighting among females, breakage of eggs and the killing of nestlings.

CANARY CAGES

Many commercially made cages are specifically made to accommodate canaries, primarily for those which are kept individually as singers. Such a cage should not be less than twenty inches long and should have three perches. It should be equipped with a spacious bathing container, which is attached to the outside of the cage at an opening in the cage wall.

Group of cages used by a breeder of Border canaries, with empty show cages lined up along the top. Note the use of partitions and outside food and water containers. Photo by H. Lacey.

These lovebird flights were constructed by a hobbyist and suspended from his basement ceiling. Fluorescent lights, which give far less heat than incandescent bulbs, are used to simulate daylight. Photo by Dr. Herbert R. Axelrod.

Opposite, top: Cinnamon yellow and cinnamon buff Border canaries.
Opposite, bottom: Zebra finches, *Poephila guttata,* feeding on hardboiled egg. Note the gravel floor of the aviary. Photo by Mervin F. Roberts.

The breeding cage for a pair of canaries should be about twenty-three inches long and eighteen to twenty inches high. Even better is a double cage of Size 2 or 3—especially for canaries of the thoroughbred Dutch and British races. Such a cage can be subdivided by the insertion from the front of a partitioning wall. For this purpose two different partitions should be available: one made of wire mesh and one of plywood. A detailed discussion of such a double cage will be given later on.

The food containers can either be put into the cage through holes cut in the wire or placed on the bottom of the cage. Food and water containers which are attached to the outside of the cage are accessible to the birds through an opening in the wire. Feeders of this type can be great time-savers if a large number of cages are to be serviced. Young male singers should be kept in specially designed individual cages during their training period. These cages are available in all-metal construction or with a wooden frame. Both have facilities for outside or inside feeding. The size is approximately ten inches by seven inches by eight inches.

Canary cages in a bird room. Note partitions, outside feeding containers, and pull-out trays. Also note heating unit for maintaining proper temperatures within the room.

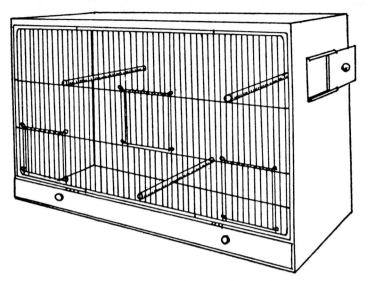

Fig. 12: Box cage. Note the location of the gates.

BOX CAGES

Box cages serve many different purposes. They are very useful for the acclimation of newly arrived birds. Because birds kept in these cages are protected from drafts, they become adjusted to the new surroundings more readily. These cages are also useful for breeding purposes for individual pairs since birds so housed are out of the sight of other birds; thus, they remain undisturbed.

A box cage consists of a simple box or crate which has wire along the front only (fig. 12). Such cages are often made of wood but are also available in light metal or various plastic materials.

While commercially made box cages are available in a great variety of sizes, shapes and materials, there may be some occasions when a desired size or shape is not available. The hobbyist then has two choices; he can adapt his needs to a commercially available cage, which is by far the more practical choice, or he can build his own box cage. Before the latter choice is made, one must consider whether

Peach-faced lovebirds, *Agapornis roseicollis,* in indoor flight cage to which nest boxes have been attached. Photo by Dr. Herbert R. Axelrod.

Opposite, top: Lovebirds perched atop nest box that has been suspended inside the enclosure. Photo by Glen S. Axelrod.
Opposite, bottom: Branches and nesting sites have been attached to the ceiling and walls of this aviary for lovebirds.

or not he has the necessary tools and skill to do the job properly. Furthermore, even if one has the tools and the skill, it may still wind up costing more to custom-build a cage than to purchase a commercially available model. If you decide to custom-build a box cage, here are a few suggestions.

The side walls and the bottom should consist of pressed wood (masonite) of about one-quarter inch thickness, laminated on both sides with waterproofed (marine) plywood of one-eighth thickness. The total thickness of the side walls and the bottom should be about one-half inch. The back wall and the ceiling can be made of the same waterproofed plywood and nailed against the side walls. To increase the sturdiness of the cage small triangular pieces of wood can be attached into the corners between the back wall, the ceiling and the bottom respectively. Along the front a piece of one-half inch by one-half inch wood extends just underneath the ceiling; this serves for attaching the front wires. Four inches above the bottom there should be another wood cross-member of identical thickness upon which the front wire rests. Along the lower cross-member a four-inch-wide hatch cover is attached by hinges; this covers the opening for the bottom tray. It is advisable to have two small hooks with which to lock the hatch cover against the cage. The bottom tray should not rest directly on the bottom but on two perpendicular, three-quarter-inch-high wood runners; this makes tray removal very easy. A tray of two inches depth is recommended. Allow about one inch between the upper edge of the tray and the lower wood cross-member; this permits a good grip on the tray when removing it. When estimating the height of the box cage, allow about three-quarters of an inch for the tray slides, two inches for the tray itself, one inch from the upper edge of the tray to the lower cross-member (which is one-half inch high)—a total of four and one-quarter inches, to which is added the height of the interior of the cage proper.

It is a good idea to install a door in one of the side walls. The bird can easily be chased through it into a smaller cage, where it can easily be caught.

The front of the cage consists of the attached wire which can be entirely wire or a hardwood frame with wire. This grate should be easy to remove so the cage can be cleaned thoroughly at any time. The distance between adjacent wire strands depends upon the kinds of birds to be kept in the cage. The front grate should have one or several doors, according to the size of the cage.

I usually place the food containers—even for softbills—on the bottom of the cage, along one of the narrow walls. For that purpose small drop-gates at both ends of the cage are quite practical so that the birds are not disturbed when food is put into the cage.

These front wires are available in different styles and sizes from cage manufacturers. A box cage must be carefully constructed, allowing no cracks or splits in the wood where parasites might breed. An interior coat of a high-quality lacquer paint—preferably in white or in bright colors—acts as a sealant for all cracks. The outside can be painted any color.

An inherent disadvantage often quoted about box cages is that they are darker than open cages. This is true to a certain degree: if they are placed where they are exposed to direct light, in front of a window, say, this disadvantage does not occur. However, when the light comes only from one side, box cages are, of course, too dark. Box cages should be placed in very bright rooms and not too far from windows. This brightens up the cage which, by the nature of its construction, tends to be rather dark inside.

Box cages are suitable for most small birds. Of the parrots one should keep only budgerigars, lovebirds and similarly small species in box cages. However, for these birds the barred cage front must be all metal, and protruding wooden supports should be covered with sheet metal.

A pair of society finches, *Lonchura domestica,* at their nesting site.
Photo by Mervin F. Roberts.

Newly hatched society finches in an open nest which has been secured to the wire mesh wall. Photo by Mervin F. Roberts.

DOUBLE CAGES

A double cage is a normal cage that has been subdivided by a partition into two compartments. Double cages are particularly popular in England as breeding cages and are commercially available as open, all-metal, hardwood frame, or box cages. The partition should be inserted from the front, which is really the only way when there are several cages side by side or on top of each other, and should be made of wire-mesh, plywood, or sheet metal. The best but most expensive partition consists of one-eighth-inch-thick acrylic or plastic. Wire-mesh partitions can be homemade or made-to-order by a cage manufacturer. The front wire of a cage must have a small opening through which the partition can be inserted.

A double cage must, of course, have a bottom tray on each side, and they should be separated by a thin vertical piece of wood or metal. This should be about one-quarter-inch higher than the edge of the tray and is meant to support the partition. Underneath the ceiling there should be a metal guide into which the partition slides. At the bottom the partition is kept aligned by screws inserted into the small pieces of wood separating the two trays. In addition, the partition wall should project about one-inch out beyond the front cage wire so it can be easily pulled out. The front wall of a double cage must have separate doors for each side of the cage to provide adequate access to both compartments. The length of such a cage should not be less than thirty inches.

A double cage can be very versatile. For breeding canaries the adults can become accustomed to each other through a wire mesh partition. A wire mesh partition is also useful to separate young birds from their parents. The young can still be fed by the parents through the wire, provided the necessary perches are attached on either side of the partition so the birds can reach each other. Double cages are also often used for hybridization between native

64

or exotic male finches and canary females, or between two different species of finches. Even for breeding small exotic birds such a cage has certain advantages. Usually familiarization between breeding partners in grass finches is no problem. However, behavioral difficulties sometimes arise with true finches, and the double cage can sometimes help solve the problem. In addition, a breeding pair can be separated from its nest by the use of a solid partition so the nest can be examined without disturbing or exciting the birds. If a cage has to be thoroughly cleaned or disinfected while it is being used for breeding, it is highly advantageous if the pair can be separated easily. Finally, catching birds—especially in larger cages—is easier to do if there is a partition.

Double cage and array of commercially available materials suitable for keeping and breeding canaries. Photo by H. Lacey.

A hummingbird comes down to a honey-water feeder attached to branches. Photo by Louise Van der Meid.

GLASS CAGES

Glass cages—also known as vitrines—have recently become popular but mainly to enhance room decor. This type of cage is less popular among most bird fanciers.

A glass cage usually has a solid ceiling and back wall made of plywood or a similar material, a front wall consisting of one or several pieces of glass, and side walls made entirely or partially of wire mesh. Often such a cage does not have a bottom tray since it is intended to depict a "mini" landscape, and the bottom is therefore covered with moss, rocks and some plants or flowers in camouflaged flowerpots. A removable tray would thus be useless. Because of this imitation landscape, maintenance and cleanliness in such a cage is difficult, although ironically it is precisely this type of cage that requires an immaculate appearance for an effective display. Another drawback is that there are usually an insufficient number of perches and branches, because they do not realistically fit into the depicted landscape. Moreover, glass becomes easily soiled and is difficult to keep clean. Unless one of the wire sides of the cage faces a window, the birds will never get direct sunlight. Often the location of such a cage is along one of the rear walls of the room, where the birds get only artificial light. All in all, a glass cage is more like a piece of furniture than a bird cage. However, one advantage of glass cages has to be recognized; food, seed shells, feathers and other debris do not fall onto the floor of the room. Birds which can justifiably be kept in glass cages are hummingbirds, other nectar feeders, white-eyes and species with similar requirements. For these species one can introduce fruit flies and other small insects into the cage. However, then the side walls and possibly also the ceiling must be covered with fly screen so that the food insects cannot escape. In addition, such screens must have doors through which food and water containers can be placed into the cages.

This elaborate glass cage was built for displaying budgies in the lobby of a Chicago movie theater during the showing of the film "Bill and Coo."

Notice the seed hoppers, thermometer, and plants in this glass cage for a group of budgies. Photo by Condit Studio.

Branches should be secured to the back wall in such a way that they can easily be replaced. They should be attached at different levels but primarily in the upper section of the cage and spaced as far apart as possible in order to leave plenty of flight space. If plants are to be kept in glass cages, supports into which flowerpots can be placed should be attached to the back wall. The side walls and the back wall should have hooks to hold water tubes for honey water and similar liquids; suction cups with hooks have proved quite useful.

The front of a glass cage consists of two sheets of glass that slide sideways in grooves. To facilitate cleaning, a third sheet can be inserted from one side while the other sheet is pulled out on the other side. For this purpose it is recommended that an opaque sheet be inserted in the middle of the cage, as suggested for double cages. In this way the birds, confined to one half of the cage, will not be disturbed while the other half is being cleaned. This is accomplished by sliding both of the glass fronts slightly to one side so that the partition can be inserted through the small opening. It is easy to increase the temperature in a glass cage by suspending an infrared heat lamp above the wire mesh ceiling.

Above: Newly shipped birds should be checked for health problems as soon as they arrive. Photo by Louise Van der Meid. **Below:** Medication may be added to the water receptacle of a hospital cage. Photo by Louise Van der Meid.

HOSPITAL CAGES

The universal treatment for ailing tropical birds is increased heat. Therefore the enthusiast should have a hospital cage that can be heated and in which sick birds can be immediately isolated.

A simple but practical hospital cage involves a box cage with a twelve-inch-square area and a height of fourteen inches. These dimensions can be changed to suit individual needs, but they are ideal for most small birds. Such a cage must be equipped with perches that run parallel to the side walls. In front of one of the perches an infrared heat lamp of 100 to 150 watts is placed outside the wire at a distance of two to four inches (fig. 13). A bird sitting on this particular perch receives the full benefit of the heat rays. Very sick birds tend to sit close to the heat lamp, but with gradual recuperation they tend to move farther away from the heat source. In this way the birds themselves can determine whether or not they wish to be exposed to high temperatures. Food and water containers are placed on the bottom of the cage, as far away from the heat lamp as possible.

The bottom of such a hospital cage is covered with several layers of newspaper; the bird droppings are thus easily monitored. Only after the bird is fully recovered is it then gradually exposed again to sand.

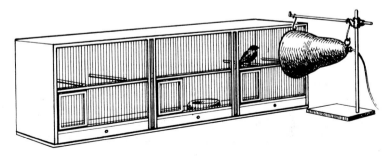

Fig. 13: A hospital cage with infrared heat lamp. At night the red light allows the bird to either leave or move into the area of heat radiation.

In this elaborate breeding facility for budgerigars, heating is thermostatically controlled and "daylight" bulbs are operated by time switches to promote breeding all the year round.

Aisles behind the cages of the same facility provide access to nest boxes. The wire cage bottoms allow waste to drop into the easily cleaned gutter. The building is a converted stable with sixteen-inch thick walls. Photo courtesy of Fred'k D. Tharby.

This indoor aviary was not built to ideal specifications; however, it does show what can be accomplished with imagination and commonly available materials. Photo by Dr. Herbert R. Axelrod.

INDOOR AVIARIES

Indoor aviaries are basically large flight cages which can be set up indoors. Such an aviary can be built either solidly against one wall of the room or as a free-standing, large cage. In rooms also used by people, the latter recommendation is preferable.

Aviary units can be bought which may be used in part or as complete units for establishing an indoor aviary. Using such units saves a lot of time, and the complete aviary invariably looks rather neat.

However, in most cases the hobbyist will have to build his own indoor aviary. Anyone who is handy with tools can do the job himself; otherwise, the various components can also be custom-built.

The following suggestions are intended as guidelines for establishing an indoor aviary. The relationship between length, depth and height should be essentially the same as that applied to cages. The length is the decisive dimension, and the height should not exceed the length. An ideal aviary is six feet long, three feet wide and four and one-half to six feet high.

The indoor aviary may be placed on supports so that the bottom is about thirty inches above the floor. This enables the hobbyist to better control and observe his birds when they are on the bottom of the aviary. It is convenient to have a small cupboard for storing food and other equipment built in below the aviary. Also, placing the entire aviary on casters so that it can be moved about makes cleaning the general area around the aviary easier. In order to facilitate cleaning the aviary an opening with a tight-fitting hatch is advantageous. Sand and debris can thus be easily swept out; the hatch does not have to be very large.

The back wall of the aviary should consist of smooth, rather light boards or plastic panels. The other three sides and the ceiling should be made of wire mesh attached to a wood frame. It is practical to screw individual frames together instead of nailing them together, so that the aviary can be dismantled easily when it is moved or repaired. The wire mesh commonly used for an aviary has an opening one-half-inch square, or one by one-half inch, with a wire thickness of 1.24 mm (fig. 14). This wire is fine enough and open enough not to interfere with viewing the birds, and it is easy to work with.

An indoor aviary should have several doors so that all areas inside it are easily accessible. In addition, there should be a large gate for introducing branches and possibly even permitting the hobbyist to climb into the aviary. The door can be in two sections which open above and below. The lower part of the door should be close to the bottom making it convenient to place food dishes on the bottom of the aviary. It also reduces the risk of birds escaping. Along the narrow sides and also along the front there can be several small gates close to the bottom through which additional food and bathing containers can be put into the aviary. This arrangement helps to keep the food and water relatively clean and the birds from being disturbed.

Small doors can also be located at different levels on the narrow sides of the aviary. These are used to fasten nesting boxes and through them, later on, any breeding activity can be observed. It is very useful to have a larger door of about eight inches square in one of the upper corners along one narrow side. This can be used, when needed, to chase birds into a smaller cage attached on the outside.

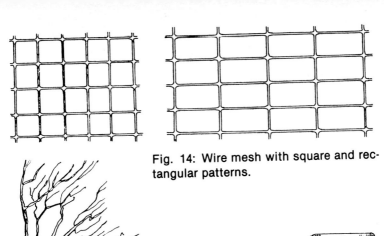

Fig. 14: Wire mesh with square and rectangular patterns.

Fig. 16: One type of clamp for attaching branches.

Fig. 15: Branches are attached with two clamps to prevent them from tipping over.

Branches are attached at various levels along the back wall, using clamps (figs. 15, 16). They are attached to the side walls by tying them to wire mesh with pliable wire. It is important that these branches not be placed directly above each other or above food containers. This prevents droppings from contaminating the food or from landing on other birds. The branches should not cover the entire width of the aviary; ample open flight space should be allowed to remain.

It must be emphasized that an aviary should not be overcrowded, and that the birds kept are compatible in size and behavior. Those species which are known troublemakers should be kept in separate cages. It is outright cruelty to house aggressive birds with those that are peaceful.

Above are parrots in all-metal cages having wire mesh bottoms for easy cleaning of droppings and seed husks. Tree branches and plants add naturalness to an indoor aviary such as that below housing cockatiels.

Whether outdoors or indoors, wire mesh should be suitable to the species being kept, whether finches and grass parakeets (above) or cockatiels (below). Top photo by Louise Van der Meid, bottom photo by Dr. Herbert R. Axelrod.

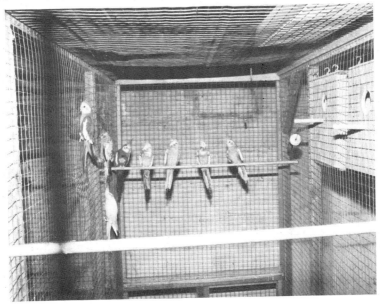

Ease of maintenance (such as placing feeding dishes at arm's level on doors) is an important consideration in constructing a bird room.

BIRD ROOMS

When establishing a bird room there are a number of general guidelines that should be kept in mind. Light and sunshine are important to the well-being of birds. Accordingly, there should be some direct sunlight entering the bird room via a window or two. A south-, southeast- or southwest-facing window admits the most suitable amount of sunshine. If the bird room is to be established in a basement, the room should have large, above-ground windows. The basement should also be well heated and not excessively damp. Attics are less suitable as bird rooms, as they tend to be too hot during the summer and too cold during the winter. However, if an attic has been remodeled and is well insulated, it could serve as a good bird room.

Several pairs of the same species or closely related forms cannot always be kept together, even if the room is large enough. Moreover, in some cases, the young will have to be removed as soon as they are independent. For that reason a bird room is usually divided into two or more aviary sections. Along one side there should be a passageway, at least one yard wide, from which the birds can be fed and observed.

Below the raised floors of the aviary sections, space should be provided for storing food and accessories. It is useful to have the floors of the aviaries extend beyond the front about fifteen to twenty inches. This provides a low shelf for preparing food and filling containers. Open cages containing birds which are to be introduced into the aviary can also be placed on this shelf. In the back of the room there should be shelves for cages, or cupboard space, which will be discussed in detail later on.

The aviaries themselves should be made of a wood framework covered with wire mesh. For frames I use planed one-inch by two-inch lumber strips. For small birds a mesh size of one-half-inch square, or one by one-half inch, with a wire thickness of 1.24 mm, should be used. The walls dividing the aviaires into sections should be made of the same wire mesh. However, if each section is to have a window, I prefer to make the dividing walls solid partitions half-way along from the windowed back wall, with mesh the rest of the way. This permits nest boxes to be fastened more securely, and the birds themselves will certainly feel more comfortable.

Notice that the wire mesh has been attached on the inside of the wooden frames and that there are mesh coverings for the windows.
Photo by Leslie Overend Ltd.

Each aviary should have an access door through which the hobbyist can enter the facility. Ideally, this door should have two sections as previously described.

Each window must have a protective wire cover. For these the same wire mesh used to construct the aviary itself can be used. The wire mesh is attached to a wooden frame that can be easily removed if the window has to be cleaned. These window covers should have small, tight-fitting hatches through which the windows can be opened and closed without difficulty. It is even better if the window can be operated through rod linkages or ropes directly from the passageway. In summer months the windows may be kept open the entire day during good weather.

If the bird room is on the ground floor, it is convenient to have a small outdoor aviary directly in front of the window. If the bird room is above ground level, a small cage attached outside the window will allow the birds to enjoy direct sunshine. Such a window aviary consists of a cage made of wire mesh bent at the various angles, with the sides held together with wire clips. The bottom can also consist of the same wire mesh, which then permits easy cleaning. However, if there is a street or path underneath, the window avairy must have a sheet metal tray as a bottom, in order to protect passersby from falling debris or droppings. The birds can enter the window aviary through a small dropgate. The window aviary does not need to be very large; I have found sizes of about thirty by twenty-five inches with a height of thirty inches quite useful. A window aviary should be equipped with perches. At dusk the birds should be driven back into the indoor aviary in order to protect them from sudden nighttime storms or predators. It is especially important that young birds do not remain outside overnight. A window aviary can have a solid roof, but if the birds are used to returning to the indoor aviary, this is not necessary.

For ease of maintenance, you will need to compromise in trying to provide a natural environment for your birds. Potted plants and large trays for seeds and water (whether for drinking or bathing) are helpful. Still, you will want to check the condition of the floor at regular intervals.

Above right: A wire mesh cage can be attached directly in front of a window to create a small outdoor aviary. **Below:** Notice that while wire mesh has been attached on the inside of the frame, mosquito netting has been fastened to the outside. Photo by Mervin F. Roberts.

A good variety of branches and nest boxes, as well as spray millet, have been supplied for the zebra finches in this bird room.

In setting up a bird room it is important that all existing wallpaper be removed and the walls simply be white-washed. Branches can be attached to the walls at different levels. In the event the room has wood walls, the branches are simply nailed to the wall. If, however, the walls are masonry, it is often easier to insert hooks to which the branches are then tied. The walls can also be lined with large wire mesh against which the branches are then fastened. Such wire paneling is practical, particularly for attaching bundles of small branches. An arrangement of this kind also enables nesting facilities to be attached without much difficulty. It is important, however, that the wire mesh be close against the wall in order to prevent the birds from being trapped behind the wire. Moreover, it is recommended that a rather large wire mesh be used, about one-inch-square or larger; this supports the weight of heavy branches better than a finer mesh would.

If the aviary is entered frequently enough, and if it is not too small, the birds get used to these visits rather quickly and are not unduly disturbed. Therefore, I like to go into the aviaries as often as possible.

A net should not be used to catch birds in an aviary. Instead, a large aviary should have a small bird-collecting compartment to which the birds are accustomed. A collecting compartment consists of a bottomless wire cage that is not too small. It is placed to surround and cover the food dishes. It has a medium-sized drop-gate, which is operated with a thin but strong rope. When the bird to be caught enters the cage, the gate is dropped immediately. It is suggested that such a cage have a second door which is always open when the cage is not used for trapping birds. The second door will prevent an aggressive bird from keeping other birds from the food. To prevent the food from becoming soiled or contaminated, a sheet of transparent plastic should be placed on top of the collecting cage. If the collecting cage is always in place above the food containers, the birds will soon get used to it. However, patience is necessary because sometimes it may take a while for a particular bird to enter. However, it may take even longer if the trap is placed into the aviary only when birds are to be caught.

Nesting facilities for finches (and other birds) may take several different forms and may be attached at different heights.

Nesting facilities should be attached at different heights along the walls. In addition to nest boxes and baskets, bundles of twigs and branches should be readily available for birds that use open nests. The bottom of the aviary should contain small bushes, straw and even small piles of stones which are often used by ground breeders.

Zebra and society finches prefer closed baskets, while the green singing finch prefers open baskets. Photo by Mervin F. Roberts.

The ground cover in these aviaries should be rather deep and consist, ideally, of river sand and forest soil. It is recommended that bathing containers always be placed in roomy sheet-metal trays, in order to keep the ground from becoming soaked. There should also be automatic drinking water dispensers for a constant supply of clean water.

The cages in this bird dealer's display can be made larger by removal of partitions. Note also the water dispensers attached to the outsides of cages. Photo by H. Lacey.

A bird room of another type contains only cages of different sizes. Such a room is frequently used when various pairs are to be kept in individual cages for breeding or observation. It is also useful for setting up a commercial canary or parakeet breeding facility. Best suited for this purpose is a room which is rather long and not too deep. Preferably it should have a window in one of the long sides. A desirable width would be six to eight feet. Shelves can be installed along the back wall to hold both open and box cages. If the fronts of the cages always face the window, there will be adequate light. If cages of different heights are to be used, the shelf levels should be adjustable. To make servicing low cages and observing the birds in them more convenient, the lowest shelf should be at least twenty-five inches off the floor. It is not recommended to have more than three rows of cages stacked on top of each other; otherwise servicing the top row becomes rather difficult.

I have found it useful to have cages built solidly against the back wall. To facilitate this, the back wall should be lined, preferably with plywood or hardboard. The supporting framework can be made of pieces of three-quarters by one-inch lumber. The bottom of the individual cage compartments can be made of planed lumber, heavy hardboard, or plywood panels. In addition, individual cages should have trays covered on the outside by a lift hatch, as described for the box cages. The front should have upright pieces of wood which permit the insertion of partition panels. This arrangement has already been described for double cages. The partitions can be made either of wire mesh or some solid material. By removing two or more partitions a very large cage can be set up (fig. 17).

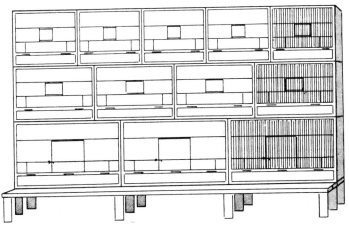

Fig. 17: Bank of cages on three levels.

An interesting pattern is seen when looking across a passageway from inside a flight. Note the openings between the outdoor and indoor sections.

OUTDOOR AVIARIES
AND BIRD HOUSES

Properly constructed and equipped, outdoor aviaries provide the most suitable conditions for the birds, as well as the best opportunities for observing them. During the summer nearly all exotic bird species can be kept in outdoor aviaries. Many of these, as well as local species, can be kept throughout the year in such aviaries. The winter months always raise a number of problems, but it is now possible to keep some species outside, provided adequate precautions are taken. Most tropical finches, as well as all insect, nectar and honey feeders and related birds, have to be kept indoors in heated accommodations during the winter. Therefore, outdoor aviaries are often established for use only during the summer months; once the weather turns cold the birds are returned indoors. The most ideal situation is one where an outdoor aviary has a direct connection to adequate indoor facilities (indoor aviary, bird room). Then the birds can be permitted to go outdoors for a short period of time on milder winter days or in early spring; thus they gradually become acclimated to outdoor conditions. An advantage with such an arrangement is that breeding pairs are not disturbed. The birds must never be forced outside but instead should have the opportunity to enter the outdoor aviary on their own. If, on the other hand, the birds are kept in cages or indoor aviaries without direct connection to outdoor facilities, they have to be very gradually acclimated to temperature changes. Moreover, there is always a delay before the birds become adjusted to their new surroundings and start to breed.

Every outdoor aviary—even those used only during the summer months—should have a completely enclosed section where the birds can seek shelter at night and during inclement weather. Corrugated transparent plastic or acrylic material is quite suitable for this purpose. It is recommended that the enclosed section of the aviary be separated from the rest by a relatively large door, which should remain open during the day. At night birds are driven into the protected section and the door is closed. In this way the birds are protected against rain, cats, owls and other dangers. They quickly become used to this procedure, and, after a short period of time, at night they tend to go into the enclosure on their own. It should be equipped with adequate perches of all kinds such as branches and twigs as well as suitable nesting facilities. This protected compartment is also very helpful to young birds which have just left the nest. In an open aviary they are very prone to accidents

One possible arrangement for outdoor and indoor sections. Photo by Charles R. Fischer.

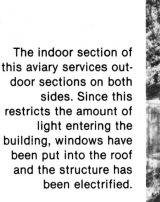

The indoor section of this aviary services outdoor sections on both sides. Since this restricts the amount of light entering the building, windows have been put into the roof and the structure has been electrified.

during thunderstorms and other adverse weather conditions. Moreover, nests are better protected here than in an open aviary. Thus I usually do not provide nesting facilities in the open section (except for parrots and parakeets, and then in the roofed-over section).

An outdoor aviary should never be placed in a completely unprotected location. One or two sides should be somewhat protected by either a wall or a hedge. Moreover, it is desirable for the aviary to be shaded from the midday sun by some trees. An aviary with direct access to indoor facilities, either in the basement or on the ground level, always has the building for protection; the same applies to an aviary which has an adjacent bird house attached to it. Yet, even this kind of an aviary should be partially roofed-over for a space about three to six feet along the house wall.

The larger the aviary, the less important the relationship between length and width becomes. However, the height of an aviary for smaller birds should not exceed six or seven feet. A rectangular shape—about nine by twelve feet for example—is preferred over a square shape.

Above: A rooftop coop for racing pigeons. The wires on the roof of the coop are to encourage pigeons to go inside the structure rather than to sit on its roof. **Below:** An L-shaped indoor-outdoor aviary for budgies. Photo by Richmond Aviaries.

Above: Another design of a pigeon coop to be compared with the structure on opposite page. **Below:** This aviary is well protected by an abundance of foliage.

97

Above: Protective wire mesh over the window is also used for attaching branches in this bird room. Cockatiel, *Nymphicus hollandicus.* Photo by Brian Seed.
Below: Feeding hatch and tray for a sulphur-crested cockatoo. Photo by John Daniel.

A pair of pearled cockatiels perched on branches in a bird room.
Photo by Brian Seed.

If one wants to keep a larger number of individual breeding pairs, a few other points must be considered. It is desirable for that purpose to build a rather long but narrow house that is subdivided into several sections. Each section should have a corresponding outdoor aviary with a roofed-over and an open section (figs. 18, 19). This type of construction has recently become popular for breeding parrots and parakeets and has proved very satisfactory. A similar

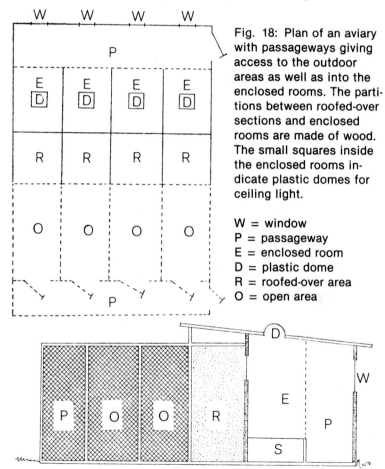

Fig. 18: Plan of an aviary with passageways giving access to the outdoor areas as well as into the enclosed rooms. The partitions between roofed-over sections and enclosed rooms are made of wood. The small squares inside the enclosed rooms indicate plastic domes for ceiling light.

W = window
P = passageway
E = enclosed room
D = plastic dome
R = roofed-over area
O = open area

Fig. 19: Cross section of facility shown in figure 18.

S = storage space beneath floor of enclosed room.

arrangement is also advantageous for breeding seedeaters and insectivores.

In a enclosed room with several sections side-by-side, maintenance is often facilitated and the risk of escaping birds reduced if one builds in a feeding passageway about three to four feet wide along the back wall of the room. This provides easy access to each section. The passageway is separated from the individual sections by a wire fence. However, the walls between the adjacent sections are made of lumber. In addition, it is often very useful to build another passage three feet wide along the open portion of a row of outdoor aviaries (figs. 18, 19) to allow easy access via doors to each aviary. With this arrangement it is nearly impossible for birds to escape. Another advantage is that if the outer sides of the two aviaries on either end are protected by sheets of transparent plastic, the birds are protected against predators.

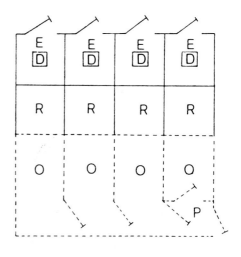

Fig. 20: Plan of an aviary built without a passageway along the enclosed rooms. Access to the open areas is handled differently from the facility shown in fig. 18.

In the case of an enclosed room having several sections but no joint feeding passage, then each section should have a small feeding hatch in the back wall (fig. 20). As a precautionary measure there should be a sliding gate on the inside

Above: Indoor and outdoor sections of a budgerigar aviary. Photo by Ray Hanson.
Below: Natural vegetation abounds in the outdoor section of this well-constructed aviary.

Above: Wire used for eleonora cockatoos, *Cacatua galerita eleonora,* should be thick and possibly even doubled (as in the roof portion of this aviary). Photo by John Daniel.
Below: Foliage may be used to camouflage wire mesh, as shown in this illustration of red-tailed cockatoos, *Calyptorhynchus magnificus.* Photo by L. Robinson.

of the wall, so that when the feeding hatch is opened, the birds cannot escape. Inside, below the feeding hatch, a board can be attached to the wall for the various food containers. But in my aviaries I use wire mesh for this purpose; it has a small bent-up edge around it (fig. 5). Unlike a solid piece of wood, this wire-mesh support for feeding dishes always stays clean and tidy because food remnants fall through to the floor.

Small doors along the back wall provide access to the aviary sections. They should be tight-fitting, to prevent any drafts. They should be placed at a height of about four feet and not be wider than twenty to twenty-five inches.

When entering a protected room, it is important to be sure that all the birds are in the outdoor part of the aviary. Therefore, there should be an additional wire door that allows looking into the outdoor part.

For pairs of larger parrots (Australian king parrot, red-winged parrot), the length of the open part of an aviary section should be about eighteen to twenty-four feet. For medium-sized species (rosellas, *Bernardius* parrots and the larger *Psittacula* species), fifteen to eighteen feet is adequate, while nine to sixteen feet will serve for smaller birds (*Psephotus* parrots, cockatiels and grass parakeets). For the less agile fliers (lovebirds, parrotlets) six feet is suitable. The widths should be five feet, four feet and three feet, respectively. A height of six to seven feet is adequate for all. Smaller enclosures having a length of six to eight feet are very useful for breeding some of the Australian grass finches. One can always keep three to five pairs in each section. Macaws and cockatoos should have an aviary eighteen to twenty-four feet long, with a width of at least six feet (but preferably nine feet) and a height of seven to nine feet.

Depending on which species will be housed, various types of wire mesh are suitable for outdoor aviaries. First of all, there is the well-known hexagonal chicken wire, with a mesh size of one-half inch. This wire is usually galvanized

Doors and windows should be strategically placed according to purpose and for convenience.

after it has been manufactured, and therefore bits and pieces of zinc adhere to it. Unfortunately, these bits of zinc are often chewed on and swallowed by parrots and parakeets and invariably cause death. Budgerigars especially are prone to doing this. This wire is very thin and is really suitable only for aviaries which do not house parrots and parakeets. Its only advantage is that it is cheap and available in various widths.

Rectangular woven wire mesh of the type used in zoos is also available to the hobbyist. This material is made from pre-galvanized wire and does not have the disastrous metal clumps adhering to it. It is available in a variety of mesh sizes, widths and gauges, but is usually rather expensive. It is particularly useful for large parrots, especially macaws and cockatoos, since these birds have a very strong beak which they use with impressive competence. For these birds a wire thickness of 2.5 mm and a mesh size of about one inch should be used.

The most suitable wire is one which is welded together and is used commonly by farmers raising fur-bearing animals. This wire has a square or rectangular mesh that is either one-half-inch square or one-half by one inch. For

Wire mesh is attached only on the inside of the wooden frames in the aviaries shown at left (housing a monk parakeet, *Myiopsitta monachus*) and below (housing a turquoisine grass parakeet, splendid grass parakeet and western rosella). Photo at left by Tony Silva; photo below by Dr. Herbert R. Axelrod.

Wire is attached to both the inside and the outside of the frame (a practice called "double wiring") in the sections of aviaries shown at right (housing a sulphur-crested cockatoo, photo by Frank Nothaft) and below (housing young Bourke's parakeets). Lower photo by Chellman and Petrulla.

The outdoor framework is made of two-by-fours. Windows above the outdoor section permit natural light to enter the indoor section.

small birds as well as the smaller parrots and parakeets, including budgerigars, a wire thickness of 1.24 mm is recommended, and for the larger parrots, from rosellas on upward, 1.65 to 2.1 mm. For outdoor aviaries the heavier wire thickness should always be used, particularly for the outer walls. This material is superb for such purposes and it is easy to work with. If door frames are covered with it, the wire does not become distorted. This wire should always be attached against the inside of the frame, including the roof.

One other point should be mentioned: All wire mesh should always be thoroughly washed with hot, soapy water in order to remove any acids or oils present.

For the framework of an aviary, including indoor flight cages and bird rooms, I prefer wood over metal. Wood always gives a lighter impression than metal and can more easily be worked by any skilled hobbyist. By the way, for indoor aviaries, pieces of two-by-four are quite suitable. Somewhat lighter material can be used for smaller aviaries.

The frame of an indoor aviary should be covered with a non-toxic paint. Initially, the wire should be attached with a few nails in order to keep it in the proper position, and thereafter it should be permanently secured with thin strips of wood nailed or screwed against the wire.

The opening between the outdoor aviary and the protected enclosure depends largely upon the shape and size of the actual aviary and the bird species to be kept in it. Parakeet aviaries which accommodate only a single breeding pair should have a flight opening which is relatively large—about 12 inches high and 15 inches wide—so the birds can fly straight through the opening from a perch in an enclosed room to one in the outdoor aviary. For that purpose the flight opening should be rather high, at about the level of the perches. Such an opening can be closed easily by means of a gate operated from the outside. Aviaries that accommodate various species should be equipped with two openings: one at ground level (especially for ground birds such as quail) and another about three feet above the bottom.

This outdoor section has been roofed over and fitted with removable windows as added protection against inclement weather.

Wood is the material most commonly used for building aviaries.
Photo by Ray Hanson.

Aviaries are also constructed of brick (as above, in an aviary housing plum-headed parakeets, *Psittacula cyanocephala)* and galvanized metal (as below, in an aviary housing cockatiels). Photo above by Dr. Herbert R. Axelrod; lower photo by Dr. Gerald R. Allen.

The adjacent enclosed rooms should not be too small. After all, the birds will have to spend a considerable amount of time in them during the winter and periods of inclement weather. An enclosure should have the same width as the open part. Its length should not be less than four feet, increasing to six to seven feet for the larger units. Its height should be the same as the outdoor part. This makes a space that is as high, or higher, than it is long or wide. Since the birds will not like to fly down to the floor, it is advisable to add a second floor, about twenty to thirty inches above the first. This makes the enclosure only about four feet high. The space below the raised floor can be used for storing a variety of foods and equipment.

The enclosed room, in most cases, is constructed of lumber. The walls should have an interspace filled with some kind of insulating material such as glass wool, which is not attractive to mice. To keep rats and mice out, the underside of the wood structures should be covered with sheet metal. While enclosured rooms which are used only during the summer months do not need double walls insulation, they must always be dry and draft-free.

Simple, straight-line construction of indoor and outdoor sections. (Note peacock displaying in foreground.)

Elaborate two-story building, well suited for a variety of pigeons.

Few hobbyists can afford to construct buildings for their birds. Whether made of brick or lumber, structural details will not be discussed here, because they depend largely on individual situations; specific advice can be provided by contractors or architects. Only the fundamental principles are given here.

Such a bird house should be of the usual room height. The walls must be sufficiently solid so that it can be kept at a desired temperature, especially during periods of extreme cold. The windows should face south, southeast or southwest. Ideally, it should be rectangular and relatively narrow. All indoor flight cages should be situated along an access passageway from which they can be easily serviced. As in bird rooms, it is recommended that the indoor flight cages be placed about 20 inches above the building's floor,

113

Aviaries may be as simple as the ones for doves on the opposite page or as elaborate as the one for pigeons shown above. Your choice of size, style, and materials is dependent upon many factors including the desired species, number of birds, area available, your ability to work with tools—and your financial resources as well.

and this elevated flight floor should be extended forward to form a shelf. The flight cages should be set up along the south wall for better heat and light. The service passage should be about four to five feet wide to make it easy to move about, possibly even containing a few chairs for sitting and watching the birds. Shelves along the north side will hold the smaller cages or a few solid cages with removable partitions. The walls between the flights can be made of lumber; this prevents birds in the various compartments from disturbing each other and also facilitates attachment of branches, nest boxes, etc. The passage is divided from the flights by the usual wire mesh.

Usually outdoor aviaries are built in front of the windows. They block out a lot of the daylight, especially if the aviaries are roofed-over with wire, glass, or sheets of plastic placed along the wall of the house. Therefore each compartment should—ideally—get daylight through a plastic roof dome. A few domes can also be installed above the service passage to provide more light. In order to determine

Plastic roof domes have been installed to provide interior light.

Above: Translucent corrugated plastic is a useful roofing material, providing protection without completely blocking out light. Photo by Glen S. Axelrod. **Below:** An outdoor flight for budgerigars, winterized with storm sash which may be removed as the weather becomes warmer.

Grass cover for the bottom of an aviary is enjoyed by many species; however, such a cover is difficult to grow and to maintain. The owner of these zebra finches solved the problem by digging up pieces of grass sod and placing them in a tray at the aviary bottom. The birds will pick up grit and also trace elements which might otherwise be lacking in their diet. Photo by Mervin F. Roberts.

An ordinary bamboo rake is an efficient device for cleaning earthen floors of outdoor aviaries. Note also the construction of this section, which proves that huge sums of money are not necessary if you have ingenuity and do not mind some hard work. Photo by Connie Allen.

the dome size, here are a few details: one dome of about twenty inches square is sufficient for a floor area eight feet by eight feet; thirty inches square for a floor area of twenty by twenty feet, and forty inches square for an area thirty by thirty feet.

It is advisable, too, to have a small food preparation area (kitchen). This can be provided with cupboards and drawers for storing food and equipment and possibly with a small refrigerator for keeping soft foods. It should also include a wash basin for cleaning food containers and equipment.

The ground cover in an outdoor aviary is of paramount importance for the health of the birds. Small aviaries that consist only of an outdoor flight area and an enclosed room can be built so they can be moved every year to a new site. Such frequent changes help to avoid infections in the birds. If a portable aviary is used, the bottom of the outdoor flight area should be covered with wire mesh in order to prevent rats and mice from entering it.

In order to avoid the undesirable consequences of decaying bottom substrate, one might build the aviary on a solid concrete foundation. This also protects the birds against predators entering the aviary through the bottom. However, concrete floors must be washed off daily for health reasons and because bird droppings are particularly conspicuous on such a smooth surface. But there is a simpler and cheaper solution to the aviary floor problem: equip it with a lumber (or similar) floor, impregnated with a nontoxic preservative, and then place the entire structure on concrete pillars about twenty inches above the ground. Whatever method is employed, however, it is necessary to place wooden brackets in the concrete to secure the aviary's superstructure. Whether the framing is made of wood or metal, it should never rest directly on the concrete. Instead, it should be kept about one-quarter inch above so that it does not deteriorate too rapidly.

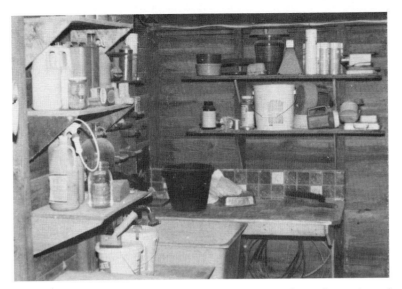

Tables and shelves are handy for storage of equipment and maintenance supplies. A wash basin or tub will be well worth the price of installation.

Smooth topsoil covers the ground in most outdoor aviaries. The soil under the perches should be cleaned as often as possible. A planted aviary should have a grass cover only in those areas where there are no perches; otherwise the grass would become soiled very quickly. All of the soil to a depth of about six to twelve inches should be replaced periodically.

An interesting solution to the soil problem—found in J. Nicolai's *Birdkeeping* (T.F.H. Publications)—is to cover the entire bottom of an outdoor aviary with a one-inch-thick layer of pine needles. An additional thinner layer is placed over this every three to four weeks. Pine needles have the advantage of keeping the bottom dry. It is not necessary to remove the needles for cleaning purposes, since the lower layers will decay in a very short period of time. Such a bottom cover also contains numerous invertebrates which are often eagerly taken by the birds.

Dr. Matthew Vriends' aviaries for small grass parakeets and larger species blend with the surrounding landscape. Note the use of natural branches in the outdoor sections as well as corrugated material for roofing over a protective area. Photo by Dr. M. Vriends.

Large zoo aviaries attempt to re-create a natural environment while affording adequate protection for birds such as this black-headed caique, *Pyonites melanocephala.* Photo by Dr. Herbert R. Axelrod.

Predator problems, especially with rats and mice, can be solved by removing the soil to a depth of 24 inches inside the aviary and then covering the entire bottom of the excavation with wire mesh flush to the foundation. The soil is then replaced in the excavation. In order to prevent the barrier wire from rusting it is recommended that it be painted with tar before replacing the soil.

In small-bird aviaries mice climbing among the branches can indeed cause a lot of damage: they disturb brooding birds and often destroy eggs and nestlings. Therefore, everything possible should be done to keep rodents out of aviaries, bird houses and similar facilities.

Another predator is the very small shrew. This insectivorous animal can squeeze through wire mesh that is even too small for mice. It can cause considerable damage and will kill everything, as martens and weasels do. Therefore, it is recommended that at least the roofed-over area of outdoor aviaries, where the birds are kept at night, be protected by an especially fine-meshed wire.

Illumination and heating for bird rooms and bird houses is essential for the winter months. Cages of the smaller indoor aviaries can be illuminated by electric bulbs. However, fluorescent lights are preferable for larger facilities.

Proper budgie cages are arranged at eye level above storage compartments. Notice that cages have plastic "seed guards" and exterior water dispensers. Photo by Louise Van der Meid.

During the winter months the day should be extended to twelve hours through the use of artificial illumination. For dusk, there is equipment available that very gradually reduces the light level so that the birds do not panic. A small night light should always be used—the birds will easily adjust to it. In the event the lights are inside the flight cages—that is, not in the feeding passage—they should always be covered by a wire screen.

Heating during the winter months must be closely controlled, especially for tropical species. Most individual family dwellings have their own heating systems that can also service the bird room.

Coal fires do not always provide the desired even temperature, and the smoke and carbon monoxide can be fatal to the birds. Anyone planning to build a bird house should give considerable thought to heating the facility. It is best that the most modern heating equipment should be installed.

For smaller enclosures, electric heat is adequate. Infrared heat lamps are very useful for this purpose. Larger facilities can also be heated with small electric heaters. Temperature should be adjustable by means of a thermostat, and all heating elements inside the flight area must be adequately covered so that the birds cannot injure themselves on them.

Portion of interior of aviary showing glassheat panels. (Keeping budgies with finches is not recommended.)

A hollow tree trunk makes a good nesting site for species such as the thick-billed parrot, *Rhynchopsitta p. pachrhyncha.* Photo by Dr. M. Vriends.

Opposite: Mourning dove, *Zenaida macroura,* on a weaver's nest suspended from the aviary ceiling. Photo by Dr. Herbert R. Axelrod.

A cockatiel and its eggs as seen by looking down into a nest box. Photo by Vince Serbin.

NESTING FACILITIES

One of the major prerequisites for successful bird breeding is that the birds be provided with suitable nesting sites. Birds in captivity do not always build their nests the same way as they do in the wild—perhaps they do not find the same conditions. Some species readily accept artificial nests, but others prefer to build their own nests among the branches of the trees and bushes in the aviary. In outdoor aviaries many birds like to build their nests among the branches of available trees. If a mixed group of birds is to be accommodated, one should provide a variety of nesting facilities and materials so as to meet the demands of the species being kept.

Parrots are less choosy than many other types of birds, as far as their nest selection is concerned. All parrots kept in captivity, with the exception of the monk parakeet, will nest in enclosed nest boxes. Nest boxes are usually made of wood, and for the more selective species hollowed-out tree-trunk sections can be used. Some parrot species (lovebirds and hanging parrots, for instance) carry their nesting materials (grass, straw, tree bark, etc.) into the nest box to build their own nests; other species do not. In the latter case, a handful of sawdust can be placed on the bottom of the box. Moist, slightly decaying wood chips are an even better choice. If very deep boxes are used, a thick layer of slightly moistened peat moss can be placed into the box and covered with grass sod upside down on top of it. Still less

This pair of budgies raised two sets of youngsters while kept in an aviary of soft-billed birds. The male is a lutino; the female is a turquoise blue opaline.

Opposite: Barrels and even garbage cans may be used as nest sites by parrots. Both photos by John Daniel.

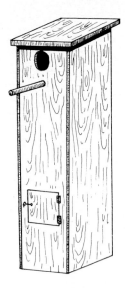

Fig. 21: Tall nest box suitable for placement on ground. The hatch for nest inspection is installed at the lower end.

demanding species can be supplied with a box having a slightly excavated wooden bottom. There should always be access from the outside via a hatch so the nest can be inspected.

For species that prefer a deep nest, one should use a cupboard-like box of about four to six feet in height (fig. 21). This box should not have a bottom and should be placed directly on the soil below the roof in an outdoor aviary. It should be filled with peat moss to a height of twelve to fifteen inches; then grass sod should be added, followed by a few handfuls of decaying wood chips. One side of the box should have a little inspection hatch. From the birds' entrance hole to the bottom a small ladder made of wire mesh should be placed to enable the birds to climb into and out of the box. This upright "starling" box is the simplest and perhaps the most commonly used box model.

In the following list of nestbox sizes for various species, dimensions in inches are given for the floor, height range, and diameter of the entrance hole, respectively.

Budgerigars, parrotlets: 7 x 7, 10—11, 1.8
Grass parakeets: 8 x 8, 12—20, 2

Red-rumped parrot: 10 x 10, 12—20, 2.5
Cockatiels, western rosella: 11 x 11, 20—24, 2.5
Eastern rosella, Port Lincoln parrot: 11 x 11, 20—24, 2.5
Australian king parrot, red-winged parrot: 11 x 11,
    40—80, 3.3

When constructing a nest box, consider whether it is to be attached to the inside or the outside of the cage or aviary. Boxes for the inside should have hinges for the roof hatch attached to the side opposite the entrance hole (fig. 22); those to be attached to the outside must have their hinges placed on the same side (fig. 23).

A similar box which is designed to be attached at an angle of about forty-five degrees against the wall (fig. 24) has also proven to be very satisfactory (the bottom, of course, must always be horizontal). Also, horizontal boxes are being used in increasing numbers. In these the entrance hole is located along the upper edge of one of the long sides (fig. 25).

Fig. 22: Simple nest box to be suspended inside a cage or aviary.

Fig. 24: Sloping nest box to be suspended against a wall.

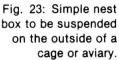

Fig. 23: Simple nest box to be suspended on the outside of a cage or aviary.

Fig. 25: One type of horizontal nest box.

133

Zebra finches in an open nest. Photo by Mervin F. Roberts.

Opposite: Zebra finches in an enclosed nest
basket. Photo by Harry V. Lacey.

Below the entrance hole, on the inside of the box, a rectangular block of wood should be attached. When entering the nest box the birds can then hop onto this platform first, rather than land directly on top of the nest.

Large empty barrels are commonly used as nest boxes for very large parrots. Frequently macaws will breed in half-opened barrels or open wooden boxes placed in one corner of the enclosed room. It is recommended for this purpose that a box be made of a very heavy hardwood (e.g., oak) that will offer some resistance to the continual chewing of these birds.

Two important points have to be observed when equipping nest boxes. The box has to meet the specific needs of a particular species as far as its size is concerned. Equally important is the size of the entrance hole. The birds will not accept a nest box if the hole is too large or too small. In cases where the hole is too large the problem can be remedied by nailing a piece of wood into which has been cut a hole that is slightly too small. The birds will then enlarge this hole to meet their own needs.

In the wild nearly all true finches build open nests. However, there are a few exceptions such as the Cuban finches and various *Sicalis* species. Small birds that build open nests are usually not very eager to accept artificial nesting sites. Instead, they prefer to build their own nests in bushes and small trees. Therefore, these species have to be provided with a variety of branches from both hard- and softwood trees nailed at different levels against the wall of the aviary, so the birds can select their own nest site. Some birds will accept open basket nests or open wooden boxes (fig. 26); these too should be available in a wide selection. Sometimes even more or less closed nest boxes are used—roller canary cages, for example (fig. 27). Most birds, however, prefer live bushes or trees such as the various evergreens, boxwood, and such.

Society finches will perch on, but probably not breed in, an open nest.

All waxbills and grass finches build enclosed nests. Certain pairs prefer to establish their nest in bushes or directly on the ground. However, many will accept artificial nesting facilities. Such enclosed nests are available in many different models, and these should be offered to the birds in an adequate selection.

Enclosed basket nests are usually accepted (fig. 28). They can be either round or rectangular. Those with wood back walls and a wood lid are preferable because they are stronger and easier to clean.

Fig. 26: Open nest basket.

Fig. 28: Enclosed nest basket.

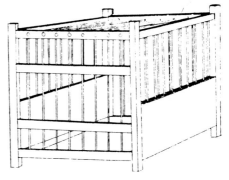

Fig. 27: Roller canary cage made completely of wood. This cage makes an excellent nest support for open as well as enclosed nests and is accepted by a variety of small birds.

137

Above: Nest log installed in a high position with perch provided near the entrance for the cockatiels' convenience. Photo by Dr. Gerald E. Allen.
Below: The log before it was hoisted up. It is about three feet long and has an opening of five inches. Photo by Dr. Gerald E. Allen.

Above: Owl finch, *Poephila bichenovi,* near nest attached to wire mesh of side wall. Photo by Ray Hanson.
Below: Painted quail, *Turnix varia,* which prefers the ground for its nesting site. Photo by Keith Hindwood.

Birds that build enclosed nests fill their nest box with a variety of materials, so the entrance hole must be of a size that allows them to carry nesting material in. Basket nests with a large entrance hole are sometimes accepted by those birds that build open nests. An enclosed basket nest should be no smaller than five inches in any dimension; a few larger nests should also be selected, since many birds, even smaller species, often prefer a larger nest.

Often, nest boxes of different sizes and models, as described for parrots, are also accepted by waxbills and grass finches. The horizontal nest box especially is eagerly taken by many species. The size should be about eight to ten inches in length and five to six inches in height and width. The wooden block below the entrance hole is not essential in these nest boxes. However, it is recommended to have a short perch (about four inches) on the outside, just below the entrance hole. Also useful are nest boxes that have a bottom six inches square and a height of about eight inches; the entrance opening should be a little less than two inches in diameter. A simple five-inch cube with a half-opened front is particularly good for cage breeding zebra finches and doves. For easy cleaning, the front or the top of the box should open.

It is always better for a nest box (such as this one for a zebra finch) to be too big rather than too small. Photo by H. Lacey.

Fig. 29: Enclosed nest made of wire mesh.

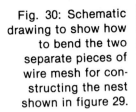

Fig. 30: Schematic drawing to show how to bend the two separate pieces of wire mesh for constructing the nest shown in figure 29.

A practical and very durable nest (figs. 29, 30) can be made of wire mesh with a mesh width of one-half inch. For a five-inch-cube nest, use two pieces of wire; one should be five by twelve inches, the other five by fifteen inches. The first piece is bent into three sections of five, five and two inches. This forms the back wall as well as the bottom, with about two inches along the front. The other piece is bent into three equal sections of five inches each. This is formed into a reverse U and so provides the side walls and the roof. These two sections are tied together with pliable wire so that a box of five inches in width, depth and height is constructed. In front of the entrance opening a small perch should be attached, preferably before the two components are connected together. This provides additional stability to the nest. A piece of styrofoam attached to the bottom completes the nest (this material is also recommended for use in wooden nest boxes). In recent years I have had very good results with these nearly indestructible and cheap nest boxes.

Among softbills there are those species that brood in open boxes, as well as those that brood in enclosed nests. The reader is referred to those details applying to other birds using similar nests.

For ground-dwelling birds (for instance quail) grass sod with long grass should be provided below bushes and along the wall of the aviary. There the birds can make the necessary excavations and establish their nests. Nesting is aided by sticking various small branches and twigs into the sod.

A sturdy platform supports the barrel used as a nest by these scarlet macaws, keeping it high in the aviary. Photo by Ray Hanson.

Opposite: Front and back views of lovebird aviaries. Photos by Tony Silva.

Pigeons make their nests out of grass, reeds, twigs, straw and coconut fibers, but such nests are usually not very durable. If the nest is built free-standing and without any support, it invariably falls down and the brood usually dies. Therefore it is imperative that adequate nesting facilities be provided to avoid such a disaster. Most suitable for larger species is a box with a wire mesh bottom (fig. 31); for birds the size of the African ring dove, a box of about six inches square, with sides two inches high, is adequate. Some moss and straw should be placed on the bottom and a few evergreen branches attached to the sides of the box. Small open boxes made of wire mesh are suitable for the smaller species such as the diamond, emerald-spotted, and harlequin doves. Just as in the case of enclosed nests, these should be made with a piece of styrofoam as a bottom cover upon which the straw and coconut fibers are placed. Some of the smaller species such as the diamond dove sometimes like to build their nests in roller canary cages. However, if birds select this site, the nest is invariably built rather sloppily. The situation can be improved by removing the nest along with the eggs and placing them inside the previously mentioned wire basket which should be placed on the roof of the roller cage. The birds usually do not object to such transfers and continue brooding in the new nest site. In order to prevent other birds from stealing nesting material, I usually sew a rim of coconut fibers around the inside of the box. For the smallest species, such as diamond, cape, and passerine ground doves, a box about five inches square is adequate.

Fig. 31: Shallow wooden box with wire mesh bottom. This makes an excellent nest support for open brooders and can be made in a variety of sizes.

Nest boxes, such as these for budgies, are normally placed high inside the aviary. Photo by Louise Van der Meid.

The location of a nest inside the aviary often has decisive significance for the successful rearing of a brood. For parrots, which are usually kept in pairs in outdoor aviaries, the nest box should preferably be suspended underneath the roofed-over section of the aviary. This protects the nest against inclement weather and permits the entry of sufficient fresh air, conditions that are of considerable advantage for parrots. Only for species that brood during the winter months should the nest box be placed inside the protective enclosed room. If several pairs of parrots are kept in the same aviary, the individual boxes should be placed at about the same height and spaced as far apart as possible. Moreover, twice as many nest boxes as breeding pairs should be offered; this avoids any arguments over nesting sites. Ideally, translucent partitions should be placed to separate the nest-box sites. In bird rooms or indoor aviaries where pairs are kept together with small birds (this usually involves the peaceful grass parakeets) the nest boxes should be suspended as high as possible, while still maintaining easy access for inspecting the nests. For finches, nests can be located all the way down to the bottom of the aviary, but never too high to prevent easy inspection. In aviaries with an adjacent enclosed room these nests are usually suspended in the roofed-over section or in the enclosed room proper.

145

Above: Lories feeding from metal tray on floor of aviary. Photo by San Diego Zoo.
Below: Dishes must be heavy to avoid being tipped over by this Hispaniolan Amazon, *Amazona ventralis*. Photo by Dr. M. Vriends.

Above: Food and water containers are available, but this young lesser hill mynah, *Gracula religiosa indica,* still prefers to be hand-fed. Photo by Louise Van der Meid.
Below: Plant saucers fill the requirements of a water dish. Photo by Dr. Gerald E. Allen.

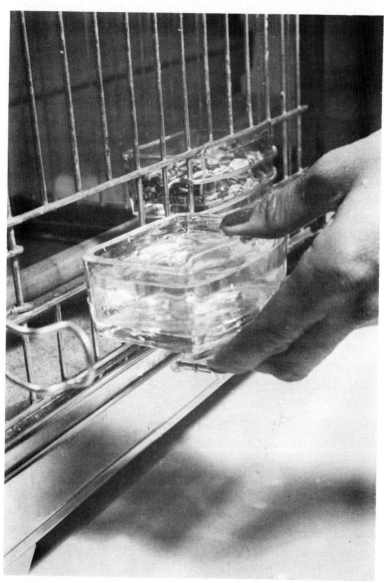
Water and food containers for a hookbill. Photo by Orlando from Three Lions.

148

FOOD AND WATER CONTAINERS

The standard food container is a small, rectangular or half-rounded dish which is inserted between the protective glass and the wire in the familiar canary cages (fig. 32). These food containers are practical if they are open at the top; this gives the birds easy access to the food. These containers are generally made of glass, porcelain, plastic, or metal. They must be easy to clean and acid-resistant. For the latter reason especially, porcelain and glazed pottery containers are preferable. Plastic containers are usually too light in weight and are tipped over quickly.

Food, including seeds, should always be placed in the container in a thin layer so the birds have easy access to the various types of food without having to dig for them. The food container should therefore be as shallow as possible. In larger bird facilities (aviaries, bird rooms, etc.) flower-pot drainage dishes can be used as food containers. Parakeets and parrots, which have a tendency to play with their food containers and often tip them over if they are too light, should be given heavy earthenware containers (such as those used by rabbit breeders).

If at all possible, each type of seed should be offered separately. Native bird seed is usually available as a mixture. However, it is recommended to also offer poppy and niger seed in separate dishes. The various softbills, whether they are native or exotic, should receive their food in

Jandaya conure, *Aratinga jandaya*. Note chewed-through wood.
Photo by P. Leysen.

A pair of superb parakeets, *Polytelis swainsonii*. Photo by Dr. Herbert R. Axelrod.

shallow dishes. In aviaries and bird rooms these dishes should be placed inside a zinc box with an edge two inches around it. This will prevent food and seed husks from being scattered throughout the entire aviary.

Automatic seed dispensers that hold large amounts of seeds and have to be refilled only about once a week are now commonly used. Such a seed dispenser consists of a container with several compartments from which the seeds slide into troughs. Often there is a tray below which collects the empty husks. The advantages of an automatic seed dispenser are obvious, but they also have a few disadvantages. Newly arrived birds or those which have just left their nest sometimes have difficulty finding the food, because they are mainly looking along the ground. Also, the trough easily becomes clogged with dust and husks and thus has to be cleaned frequently.

In small cages water is usually stored in containers similar to those used for seeds (fig. 33). Modern plastic water dispensers, which consist of a transparent tube and a lower drinking trough (fig. 34), are also quite practical. The water should be renewed every second day, and the water container should then also be cleaned.

Fig. 32: Porcelain food or water container, several types of which are commercially available.

Fig. 33: Model of an open food or water container.

Fig. 34: Modern plastic water dispenser.

Fig. 35: Birdbath made of metal frame with glass sides, to be suspended in front of cage gate.

It is often said that birds can be left unattended for several days if they are supplied with an automatic water dispenser. In my experience birds should never be left unattended for several days. However, if it is necessary to be absent for some time, it is advisable to have at least two such water dispensers in a cage or aviary.

Most birds like to take a bath. Therefore, they should be given an opportunity to do so daily in the form of a so-called bathing container suspended from outside the cage door. These containers are usually made of glass in a metal frame (fig. 35) or, more recently, of plastic. Simple bowls, such as those used underneath flowerpots, placed on the cage bottom, are also suitable.

In aviaries and bird rooms, drinking water is offered in the customary poultry drinker made of metal or plastic. Bathing water is offered in shallow earthenware dishes placed on a spacious sheet-metal tray. Of course, the ideal solution is a flowing water supply in indoor as well as outdoor aviaries.

The most important point to remember as far as drinking water and bathing water is concerned is that it must always be clean and must not be soiled by bird droppings; otherwise the danger of an infection among the birds becomes quite real.

153

Swainson's toucan, *Ramphastos swainsonii*. Photo by P. Leysen.

154

Alexandrine parakeet, *Psittacula eupatria*. Photo by Dr. Herbert R. Axelrod.

Index